Picking Up The Pieces

Moving Forward After An Abusive Relationship

Written by
LATEKA STARNES - COUNCIL

Copyright © 2021 Lateka Starnes - Council

All rights reserved.

ISBN: 978-0-578-88683-1

DEDICATION

This book is dedicated to my parents Thurman & Dorothy Starnes thank you for the love and support. My sister's Demetri, Jessica and Latesha Starnes thank you for all the laughs. My children Imanee, Imaree and Zaniyah you are my world. My nieces Kay'la and A'Niya thank you for the love and support. My G Latoya Johnson thank you for the support. My husband Christopher I want to thank you for the support, motivation and for loving me unconditionally. ANYONE that has found their self-picking up the pieces. The storm doesn't last long and the puzzle can be fixed.

Table of contents

INTRODUCTION vii
CHAPTER 1: 1
CHAPTER 2: 9
CHAPTER 3: 17
CONCLUSION 23
ABOUT THE AUTHOR 25

INTRODUCTION

He hit you again! This time, harder than he did the time before. Your head is throbbing, your eyes are swollen. Pain sears through your brain blurring your vision. The tears that have welled up in your eyes threaten to fall quickly. You are hurting but the pain you feel is not just from the cuts and bruises that have crisscrossed your face and left you scarred. This was not the fairytale you dreamed about, this was not the love and bliss he promised before you moved in together—you are crushed—but you keep asking, where did all the charm go?

Right now, you are simply tired. You are tired of wearing too much makeup to desperately cover up the bruises and the black eye he constantly gives you. You are tired of telling people that you missed your step and fell down the stairs. You are tired of always wondering what you did wrong. You are tired of explaining yourself to everyone. In the depths of your heart, you are afraid and if you have kids, you now fear for their safety. You are scared that he might hurt them or take them away from you. You are scared that they might see him hitting you and grow up thinking that's okay.

Time and again you wonder when this is going to end. You don't know how bad it's going to get and you can only wonder if your life is going to get any better. And just when you think you've had it bad; it gets worse—it's almost like he invents newer ways to be meaner each time.

Eventually, you feel alone. You feel no one truly understands what you are going through. You wish that you could just close your eyes and it will be over. On some days, you pretend to believe in magic wands. Like Cinderella, you wish that your fairy godmother will show up and everything will be alright. But you know that that's not happening—you know that are stuck in this for the long haul.

Despite the hell you've been through, you feel you deserve better. You just won't let this life be your reality! If you have kids, you'll surely want a better life for them especially if your parents went through the same cycle. You've finally had enough! You are now more determined than ever to protect your mental health at all costs. You want to be able to walk around your house without looking over your shoulder.

Now, you want to be with someone whose gaze won't make you flinch. How do I know that? Because you are reading this book right now. You are reading this book because you want real answers. You want to know what to do with yourself after threading the darkest depths of hell. You want to know if there is any hope of a decent life for you too. You want to know if you've made the right decision and if you won't end up regretting that move. The simple answer to all your questions is you've made the best decision of your life and I will walk you through why that is, but first, some perspective.

According to the National Sexual Violence Resource Center (NSVRC), approximately 1 in 4 women in the United States have experienced rape, physical violence, or stalking by an intimate partner in their lifetime. This means that millions of women have gone through something a lot similar to what you are going through and have felt the way you feel right now. Like you, these women have been bruised, disregarded, talked down at, or even totally ignored.

These women are from diverse backgrounds but all have similar experiences with abusive partners. Rihanna, a multiple Grammy award-winning singer, actress, and businesswoman was abused by her partner, Chris Brown. They always showed up at events together looking all glammed up and people gushed at their photos remarking what a fantastic couple they were. No one knew the hell Rihanna went through until photos with a black eye surfaced on the internet. In one of the interviews she granted, she said that she just had to realize that she couldn't do this anymore. Staying in that relationship wasn't just hurting her, it was hurting millions of girls who were watching. That was when she got the courage to open up about it and leave.

I cannot imagine how difficult it must have been for her to open up about the violence she was experiencing in her relationship. Many people assume if they were more beautiful, influential, or made a lot of money their partners would not be so cruel to them but Rihanna's experience showed us that these myths are not true at all. She was rich and popular but she still suffered abuse. Interestingly, she isn't the only celebrity to experience abuse. Halle Berry's ex-boyfriend hit her till she had a partial hearing loss in one ear. Mariah Carey, Madonna, and Janet Jackson also suffered abuse from their partners. These are beautiful and famous women that many adore and they have been in your shoes.

Think about all these people I've talked about. Think about how hard it must have been for them. Then, think about their lives today. See how very different things are for them now. Many of them are living beautiful meaningful lives. They have been able to put their ugly past behind them and create the future they deserve.

Today, Rihanna is a successful businesswoman and a multi-million-dollar brand. She created an all-inclusive beauty and lingerie brand–Fenty. She's worth $600 million now. Last year, Forbes named her the richest self-made woman in America. Halle Berry is a successful actress. Madonna, Janet, and Mariah Carey are successful musicians. They have global recognition; they have also won multiple awards.

Do you know that what you are going through is not very different from what they went through? Now, imagine having a life as wonderful as the one they've created. Imagine chasing your dreams, calling the shots, and living life on your own terms. Imagine not having to walk around on eggshells in your home. Imagine living free without having to look over your shoulders. Imagine living in a place where you are valued, loved and you have peace. That's what this book is going to do for you.

You may be wondering how I can guarantee all that. It's because I have been in your shoes. Like you, I have been hit, assaulted, threatened, harassed, talked down at, and treated with the greatest disrespect. More than that, I have also undergone trainings and gotten relevant education so that I could help people deal with this. Ever since I left my partner, all I have wanted to do is to help young girls and women who are going through abuse.

I know how badly bruised I was and how the entire experience affected my self-esteem. So, I made it my life's mission to save as many women as possible. I took some courses, underwent some training, and became an educator. Today, I have helped lots of women get out of these situations and go on to live meaningful lives. Many of them pursue a career, start up a company and also get into loving relationships.

They are now able to pick up the pieces of their lives and move forward from their past traumatic experiences. Would you like your life to be different like ours have? Would you like to experience peace and true happiness? If your answer is yes then, you need to commit to reading this book—every day. Read a few pages a day and internalize what you are reading. Then, participate in the self-exploration exercises.

When you are ready, turn the page. Your path to freedom has already begun.

CHAPTER 1:

A SIT DOWN WITH YOURSELF

Abuse comes with so much pain and the only way to deal with it is to confront it by sitting down with yourself. A sit down with yourself is a moment of self-reflection and brutal honesty. You have to tell yourself the truth about your situation without mincing words. This makes it easier for you to pick up the pieces and move forward. Many women who suffer abuse have a distorted reality of what they are going through. They think that the abuse is something they brought on themselves. This makes it harder for them to get out of the relationship or seek the help they need.

Adrienne's story illustrates this perfectly. When Adrienne started dating Rob, their relationship was like a fairytale. Rob was the kindest guy she had ever met. Soon, they moved in together. Rob had a high-paying job while Adrienne volunteered at the hospice center. Years later, Rob lost his job and his attitude changed. He became hostile towards his family and friends. He also became verbally abusive.

One morning, he head-butted Adrienne. Stunned, her head swirled till she saw stars. Then he said, "If you didn't talk like that, this wouldn't have happened." Those words made Adrienne feel like she was responsible for how he acted. Years later, she would still say: Maybe if I had been more supportive, or understanding or if I hadn't talked back, this wouldn't have happened.

Adrienne's story is similar to what many women go through. Their relationship starts out beautifully like a well-scripted romantic movie only to turn sour weeks down the line. Because they hold on to the idea of that romantic man they fell in low with, they don't realize that he has changed. This is why when he blames them for the things he is doing, they believe him because they think that he is too sweet to hurt them. Sadly, some women have been badly hurt believing that.

You should realize that what has happened to you is not something that you brought on yourself. It was not what you said or what you did. Rather, this was done to you by someone cruel – someone who didn't love you.

Recognize What Happened

In order to move forward, first, you need to recognize that you have been abused. If you don't recognize that, you will not be able to move forward.

You have been abused if:

- Your partner has ever hit, insulted, or humiliated you.
- Your partner feels entitled to your body/touches you without your consent.
- Your partner pressures, manipulates, or forces you into having sex.

When your partner is abusive, they tend to blame you for their behaviors. They also tend to withdraw emotional support from time to time to make you feel like you did something "wrong". They get possessive and act jealous. Sometimes, they deny their previous actions or trivialize your needs and feelings.

Abuse isn't only physical. It could be emotional. You should note this because it can be difficult to tell if your partner is abusive especially if he hasn't really hit you yet. And like we would soon see; most physically abusive relationships start with an emotional abuse.

Let's take a look at Claudia's story. Claudia met her ex-boyfriend at a restaurant where she worked. A couple of weeks later, they became a "thing" and moved in together. When he started abusing her, it wasn't physical abuse. He would embarrass her in front of people. He would tell her she was ugly and fat. Then, he would tell her that she was unlovable. He always tried to make her feel lucky to be with him. He constantly criticized everything she did. Nothing she did was good enough.

He kept doing this until she started believing him. She started feeling like she wasn't worthy of love. She started feeling ugly and thinking that she was not good enough. She now dreaded socializing or posting her pictures on social media. Her self-esteem had been battered. It wasn't long after, he started hitting her. Getting her to understand that there was nothing wrong with her was difficult. His words had sunk deep into her subconscious and altered her perception. It took months of intensive therapy, mindfulness, and meditation to help her realize that she was the victim. When she did, she left him and started moving forward.

Like Claudia's story, you may be suffering from abuse without realizing it. If your partner insults you or makes you like you don't deserve him, you are in an abusive relationship. It doesn't matter if he's rich, famous, or good-looking and you are some small-town sales attendant no one knows about. If your partner keeps making you feel inferior or unworthy of him, you are in an abusive relationship.

Here are two quick ways you can identify emotionally abusive relationships:

- If you find yourself sugar-coating his behavior when

narrating a past event to friends or family, this might be a sign that he's not treating you right.

- If you find yourself trying so hard to live up to your partner's often erratic expectations, this might mean that your relationship is abusive.

Forgiving Yourself

As you have gone through this section, you need to ask yourself, have I been abused? What abusive signs or pointers do I recognize from my past relationship. Forgive yourself and make a promise to yourself never to get in that position ever again. When you have recognized what has happened, the next thing to do is to forgive yourself. Forgiving yourself does not mean that what has happened is your fault. It only means that you are choosing to let go of all the guilt you feel.

Letting go of the guilt you feel includes forgiving yourself for the careless choices you made. Perhaps you felt that something was off from the get-go. Everything about him seemed too good to be true. And as you were packing your things to move into his apartment, you had this feeling that you couldn't shake off. You ignored it and moved in with him and weeks later, he started hitting you. You need to forgive yourself for ignoring your gut feelings. You were not crazy or stupid. You were just being human. And sometimes we trust our emotions more than our gut feelings. Sometimes, we make mistakes and trust the wrong people.

As you forgive yourself, promise that you will never get into this position ever again. This means that you will not ignore red flags or your gut feelings. You will also pay attention to what your well-meaning friends and family say. Of course, this is not to say that you would always accept their advice. It just means that you would consider it because they care about you and are looking out for you.

Cut Off The Abuser From Your Life

After forgiving yourself, you need to cut all ties with your abuser. You cannot move forward from abuse with your abuser lurking around. If you need immediate assistance, contact:

- National domestic violence hotline: call 1-800-799-SAFE (7233)
- National dating violence hotline: call 1-866-331-9474, text "loveis" to 22522
- Sexual assault hotline: call 1-800-656-HOPE (4673)

1. Cut off communication: The most effective way to cut off from your abuser is to cut all communication with him. Block and Delete his number. Block him on all social media platforms. Erase all his contact info from your phone. Delete all his text messages. Erase your chat history.

2. Get a restraining order: If your abuser is stalking you or has threatened to kill you in the past, get a restraining order. Request that the restraining order includes a distance requirement. Before getting a restraining order, find out how these restraining orders are enforced in your neighborhood. Does the violator get a jail sentence or community service? Does the abuser just get a talking-to? If your abuser just gets a warning, he may become angry and try to make things worse for you.

Keeping Yourself Safe

You may need to relocate so that your former partner can't find you. It is always best to relocate to a place he won't expect you to go. You may also need to switch your children's schools so that your abuser will not have access to them.

Here are a few tips to help keep your new location safe:

- Use prepaid phones or unlisted landlines.
- Apply to your state's address confidentiality program.
- Use a post office box rather than your home address.

Exercises

a. Like we saw in this chapter, recognizing what has happened, forgiving yourself, and cutting off your abuser are essential steps towards picking up the pieces and moving forward. Here are a few affirmations to remind you of what we've said.

Affirmations:

- I am not responsible for what my partner did.
- I am not responsible for his abusive tendencies.
- I may be bruised and broken but I'm beautiful.
- I didn't deserve what happened to me.
- I choose to let go of every guilt.
- I am cutting off from my abuser.
- I am choosing to move forward.

b. Have a 15min or 30 min sit down with yourself. Go over your relationship. Recognize what has happened and how you have been abused. choose to forgive yourself for every time you ignored your gut feeling.

c. Take a journal if speaking your thoughts out loud would be difficult for you.

d. Make plans to cut off all ties with your abuser. Make a list of your Do's and Don'ts. Involve your kids in this process.

CHAPTER 2:

TAKE ACTION

Like we emphasized previously, abuse can happen to anyone. Abuse can also be perpetrated by any man–regardless of whether he's an alcoholic, a drug user, or not. Some men are "better" hitters sober than when they are drunk/high. Abuse does not always happen because a man has a mental illness like some women believe. Abuse happens because the abuser loves to wield control over women.

When abuse does happen, it's important to take action as soon as you recognize that you are being abused. Like we stated in the previous chapter, in order to move on, it's best for you to forgive yourself and cut off from your abuser. If you don't cut off your abuser, chances are that the abuse will happen again and again. "But he's good to me most of the time," some women say.

It does not mean that he loves you. It is a tactic to keep you where he wants you. Experience has shown that abusers tend to follow up abuse episodes with generous acts so that the victim starts thinking that they were overreacting. Wanda's story illustrates this clearly. Wanda's relationship with Fred was just perfect – until one day, he threw a hammer at her. Immediately afterward, he walked right across the street and got a box of chocolates, a bottle of wine, and a bouquet of flowers. "I'm sorry," he said, "I don't know how I got so mad. It won't happen again."

Although she was stunned and in a lot of pain, she accepted his apologies. From that moment, things changed. He started abusing her constantly. He abused her emotionally and hit her from time to time. One time, he abused her sexually. Each episode of abuse was usually followed by a nice treat or flowers. Gradually, she became used to it. She would always look at him in the light of the good times they had shared. And so, she would see the abuse like regular mistakes.

One time, he threw a knife at her. That was when she knew she had to leave. Like in Wanda's story, your partner may be very good to you sometimes. They may also carry out grand gestures after every abuse episode. This doesn't mean that they are remorseful or that they are planning to change.

Feeling sympathy for or emotional attachment towards your abuser distorts your perception and puts him in charge every time. It also holds you back from taking necessary action. This puts you and your kids at risk of more harm. So, it's best to take action and start taking steps towards moving forward now.

Don't Compromise On Your Mental Health

After enduring abuse for any length of time, you need to ensure that your mental health is not compromised. This is because abuse usually has a wide range of negative impacts on a person's mental health. The American Psychiatry association in 2019, stated that approximately 20% of domestic violence survivors started experiencing psychiatric disorders such as major depressive disorder, generalized anxiety disorder, and posttraumatic stress disorder, and a wide range of substance use disorders.

Danielle's story adds some perspective to this. One night, as Danielle was sleeping, she noticed that she was having difficulty breathing. Gasping, she woke up to find her partner choking her. He stopped. The next day, she packed her things and made to leave but he pointed a gun at her daughter. She couldn't watch him shoot her. So, she stayed with him.

Out of fear, she lived with him for years. At that time, he controlled everything she did. He wouldn't let her go out with friends. He wouldn't let her go shopping except he accompanied her. He would drop her off at work and drive her home. He came to her workplace from time to time to see if she was there. Worst of all, he constantly threatened to shoot her child whenever she disagreed with him.

One day, she woke up to find that her daughter was bleeding. He shot her and disappeared. Luckily, the bullet only grazed her skin and she healed quickly. Although they had moved to another town and were now safe from the abuser, she still suffered from the effects of her experience. When she was speaking with a mental health advocate, she said, "Abuse has changed me. I can't eat. I can't sleep. I'm always afraid of what might happen next – of what might happen to my daughter. When I remember how I nearly lost her, I have difficulty trusting people—and it's ruining my friendships."

Danielle had to see a psychiatrist who gave her some medicine for anxiety. She also underwent therapy. After several sessions, she began to make progress. Now, she feels safer, is willing to give people a chance, and is hopeful for the future.

Like we saw in all the illustrations above, abuse distorts your perception and gets you to see things differently. Thus, you tend to feel insecure, less confident, unworthy, and unlovable after enduring abuse. You may also feel guilt or blame yourself for what happened. For some people, they feel fear and anxiety. They are constantly looking over their shoulder in order to preempt and forestall attacks. Some others lose the drive to live and resort to self-loathing.

As soon as you leave an abusive relationship, your first priority should be to assess your mental health status. You need to know how badly your experience has affected you and get help fixing it. To do that, you need to check in with a psychiatrist for an evaluation. The psychiatrist will ask you some questions, administer tests and decide whether you need a prescription. Your psychiatrist might also recommend counseling and support groups you can join.

In addition to checking in with the psychiatrist, you need to stay around a caring and supportive community. Having a group of caring and supportive people to closely relate with reminds you that people are not all evil. It helps to restore your faith in people and in human relationships. It also keeps you from isolating yourself and spending long hours brooding and processing negative thoughts.

Finally, you need to engage in activities. Getting busy keeps your mind off your problems and helps you channel your energy into something more productive. If your abuser stopped you from work, get a job, or try learning a skill. Do something creative. Practice your hobbies: even if they are hobbies you left off because your abuser won't let you out of his sight. Many survivors find that journaling helps them. Some other survivors have found that channeling your emotions into words, music, dance, music or art can help you work through your trauma and move forward easily. You can also try volunteering. Some women have found that helping others makes them feel better about themselves and helps them heal.

Seek Professional Help For Your Addictions (Substance Abuse or Other Addictions)

If you have any addictions (substance abuse or any other addictions), you will need to seek professional help. Therapists are trained and certified to help you go through trauma and deal with any addictions you're experiencing. They provide confidential non-judgmental interactive treatment sessions. And they help you explore thoughts, feelings that you may be unwilling to share with anyone else.

Here's a guide to how you can select a great therapist:

- Personality: Since you will be spending time with them and sharing some of your deepest secrets, you need someone with whom you can relate freely with. This means that you don't have to go along with the first therapist you speak with—except you really want to. It's okay to speak with a few and then choose.

- Experience with addictions among people who have been abused: Since you need help with addiction, it is helpful to find a therapist who has experience in that area. When you meet a therapist who you think will be a good fit for you, ask about their experience working with women like you. Ask them what approach they took and how they were able to help them overcome their addictions.

- Approach: Different therapists help you handle your issues differently because there are different approaches to helping people through addictions. Some therapy sessions involve lots of talking while some others involve mindfulness or journaling. Feel free to ask your prospective therapists about their approach to therapy and see if it's something you would be comfortable working with.

To find a therapist, call the Substance Abuse and Mental Health Services Administration Helpline at 1-800-662-HELP (4357) or check mhanational.org.

Exercises:

In this chapter, we saw that you need to take action, safeguard your mental health and seek professional help for your addictions. Here are some affirmations to remind you of what we spoke about in this chapter.

Affirmations:

- I am going to take action.
- I will prioritize my mental health.
- I surround myself with people who care about me.
- I get a job/learn new skills.
- I channel my emotions towards creativity.

- I engage in old hobbies and learn new ones.
- I will see a therapist to help with my addictions.

a. Write out a few creative activities you enjoy or have enjoyed in the past.

b. Make plans to take your kids out for a fun family time.

Call the substance abuse helpline and get in touch with a therapist.

CHAPTER 3:

SELF CARE & RECOVERY

When you have undergone abuse, practicing self-care can be challenging. This is because you may have been insulted and humiliated for so long that you start to internalize your abuser's negative words. It gets worse when you have to deal with people (close friends, family, and people you hold in high esteem) who act like the abuse was your fault. In this chapter, we will be looking at how you can love yourself, deal with judgmental people and learn to love again.

Learning To Love Yourself After Battling Abuse

Many times, we judge ourselves too harshly for not leaving the relationship sooner or for not getting help quickly. We may also get mad for not recognizing the warning signs and staying away. You need to realize that when you judge yourself, you are not going to rewrite the past or undo your previous choices. Instead, you are hurting yourself further and this will affect your healing process.

Rather than judge yourself, show yourself kindness. Pretend that this is your loved one experiencing abuse. She just told you how she has been feeling – how she has been abused. She has also been too ashamed to speak to anyone about it. Wouldn't you show empathy? Wouldn't you remind them that they did the best they could at the time? If you would, then, extend the same kindness to yourself.

Here are a few tips to guide you:

- Get in touch with your feelings: One of the things an abuser strips away from you is the ability to trust your feelings. By constantly telling you that you are crazy or that you are overreacting, it's easy to question your feelings. The surest path to recovery is reclaiming your feelings and honoring them. Journaling and meditation are great ways to explore your feelings and get acquainted with them again.

- Celebrate yourself: Think about things you are great at – and the things you have been able to do. Then, give yourself as many pats on the back as possible. More than that, write them out and frame them so that you can be reminded of how amazing you are.

- Affirm yourself every day: Take back control of your confidence and self-perception with daily affirmations. Speaking words as simple as: "I am powerful", "I am lovable", "I am beautiful" can restore your faith in yourself and help you move forward quickly.

- Set personal boundaries: Decide what you'll allow people to do and what you want. Ensure that you put measures in place to enforce them. You could communicate some of these boundaries to someone close to you – so that they can hold you accountable.

Dealing With Naive, Insensitive, Self-Righteous People

People who don't know want it's like to be abused often judge women who suffer abuse harshly. They tend to make light of an abusive woman's situation. They say things like, "If she's so uncomfortable, why won't she just leave?" They don't realize that how much power the abuser has over his victim. They don't see how badly abuse affects the victim's mind and alters their reality.

Some others may ask, "What did you do to make him so mad?" They don't realize that abuse is never about what you did but about his choice to hurt, disrespect you, and treat you like he never had any love for you at all. When you deal with people like that—especially close friends and family—realize that many times, they mean well. They are just naïve, insensitive, and ignorant. They don't understand what it means to go through abuse.

A little schooling will do them a world of good but you may not be well-equipped to do that. So, let them be. You just need to keep reminding yourself that they mean well—but you also need to give them a bit of space too. Also, don't discuss intimate details with them. Find other supportive people you can confide in. You don't need people judging you for something you had no control over. Rather, you need people who will show empathy and help you heal.

Living With A New Partner After An Abusive One

As you heal, your heart begins to learn to trust again. In time, you will meet someone new who ticks your boxes and you may want to move in with them. When that happens, although the relationship is going great and he's kind, you may notice that you still feel some fear. Maybe when you've done something you think will upset him or when he backs you into a corner when you are both running around the house, memories of how your ex- treated you come rushing back. When that happens, you may freeze up – or start hyperventilating.

How do you deal with this?

- Be sure to tell your new partner about your previous relationship so that he doesn't get overwhelmed when

things like this happen.
- Remind yourself that your new partner is nothing like your ex.
- Tell your partner about your triggers so that he can avoid them.
- Seek counseling with a therapist.
- Practice meditation and mindfulness.

As you practice these steps, allow your body to heal at its own pace. Don't rush the process or be too hard on yourself. Instead, think about the progress you are making and the beauty, peace, and joy you will gain from your new relationship.

Exercises:

a. In this chapter, we looked at self-care and recovery and we saw tips on how to love yourself, deal with naïve people and learn to live with a new partner. Here are some affirmations to remind you of what we spoke about in this chapter.

Affirmations:
- I choose to love myself.
- I choose to affirm myself every day
- I choose to celebrate my goodness.

- I refuse to listen to people who judge me.
- I open up my heart to love my new partner.
- I practice mindfulness and meditation.
- I will see a therapist to help me navigate my negative feelings.
- Write out fifteen things you love about yourself.

b. Write out all your personal boundaries and how you plan to enforce them.

CONCLUSION

You did it. You kept your word and read this book from start to finish. I must say that I am incredibly proud of you. I trust that you have been practicing the exercises that were outlined in the book and they have been helpful.

In this book, we dealt with how you can deal with the aftermath of abuse, pick your pieces, and move forward. We looked at different issues ranging from how you can confront your uncomfortable situation, to how you can recover and move forward. We were also able to answer—with the help of illustrations—a few questions you may have had concerning leaving your partner and moving forward with your life.

I hope that this book has been a tremendous resource to you. I want to encourage you to read it over and over and practice everything we have talked about. Remember to give yourself time to heal.

Don't rush the process.

Feel free to reach out to me if you have any questions or you need help readjusting to life after leaving your abusive relationship. I am waiting to hear from you.

I wish you all the best!

ABOUT THE AUTHOR

Highly resilient and passionate, Lateka Starnes-Council is a spearheading woman who has demonstrated that even when you are dealt a poor hand of cards, you can still win the game. As the proud author of Living with PTSD and founder of Soothing Serenity Baths & More LLC, Lateka leverages her dark past and experiences involving PTSD, MST, and Anxiety to empower others on their journey towards living the fulfilled, quality-driven life they deserve.

Growing up in a large family, Lateka discovered early on the true meaning behind commitment, loyalty, and the power of working hard. These core principles became the catalyst for her to join the Navy, where she served for 8 years and partook on 3 deployments. During this time, Lateka faced intense military sexual trauma, leading her to encounter the mentally taxing hardships that she still copes with today as a disabled navy veteran. However, this trauma inspired Lateka to reach out and support others facing the same/similar situations and prove that the only way to grow from past challenges is to tackle it head-on.

Fast forward to today, Lateka wrote a book on PTSD, started a non-profit organization called BE Lyfe: Life After Domestic Violence, and openly raises awareness on domestic violence, military sexual trauma, and mental illness. Furthermore, as a person who suffered from fibromyalgia and endometriosis pains for 15 years, Lateka established Soothing Serenity Baths & More LLC with the underlying mission to give others the most opulent CBD skincare products on the market so they can achieve the same life-enhancing outcome as she did.

Whether it be through her publications or her business, nothing makes Lateka happier than using her story to build others up and help them thrive. She has a genuine ardency for what she does, developed her business on a foundation of authenticity, integrity, and trust, and is devoted to instilling positive change through her dynamic efforts. Overall, Lateka believes that everyone deserves happiness, and sometimes those debilitating, heartbreaking experiences in life are the very stepping stones that can lead you down a path to something quite beautiful.

Lateka wholeheartedly enjoys giving people the ideal resources they need to look and feel their best. But aside from managing Soothing Serenity Baths & More LLC, you can also find her studying to become a future esthetician and being a loving wife and mother to three daughters.

www.ingramcontent.com/pod-product-compliance
Lightning Source LLC
Chambersburg PA
CBHW050708160426
43194CB00010B/2048